THE HYBRID MAN

THE HYBRID MAN

DONALD L. BELLILE

Order this book online at www.trafford.com
or email orders@trafford.com

Most Trafford titles are also available at major online book retailers.

Printed in Victoria, BC, Canada.

ISBN: 978-1-4269-3209-0 (sc)

ISBN: 978-1-4269-3134-5 (e-book)

*Our mission is to efficiently provide the world's finest, most comprehensive book publishing
service, enabling every author to experience success. To find out how to publish your book,
your way, and have it available worldwide, visit us online at www.trafford.com*

Trafford rev. 5/13/2010

 www.trafford.com

North America & international
toll-free: 1 888 232 4444 (USA & Canada)
phone: 250 383 6864 ♦ fax: 812 355 4082

To: The dedicated Nurses, Nurse Practitioners,
and Doctors who have given me much care.
Also
To: Thoratec Corporation which made it possible.

CONTENTS

Dedication   v

Preface   ix

My Story   1

The LVAD   29

Bonus Social Thoughts   45

Glossary*   53

Locations Of LVAD Centers   57

PREFACE

This book is a must read for the five million people across the nation who are suffering from congestive heart failure. (And, that five million is expected to double in the next 30 years with more than half a million new cases diagnosed every year.) A must read for all medical people, especially general practitioners and cardiologists. Others who would benefit from reading this book are politicians and people of all ages. This is a book that is not only informative, educational, live saving, and morally uplifting, but also entertaining with much humor as I have included some of my life stories. You will also find my thoughts about society and government that probably are quite similar to the thoughts of all those who read this book. And, yes, it wouldn't hurt for young people to read this book because it is a book about a young man's life of trials, tribulations, and the will to persevere. The younger man is now an older man living today due to a Left Ventricular Assist Device (LVAD) in his heart.

This LVAD pump has prolonged my life thus far by two and a half years. The prognosis for at least another nine years looks good at this time. All other things going well, perhaps, a new and improved pump will be available in ten years. My quality of life at the present time is very good with few limitations. The pump has provided me the opportunity of rejoicing in the births of two more grandsons. You will need to bear with me, as I am not a professional writer. No one, except myself, is doing the writing of this book. (No ghostwriter is involved for sure.) Like most of you who read this book I am just a novice at writing. I am writing from my heart! I want to convey information to all those with severe heart disease and to those loved ones or friends who have it. Don't let your general practitioner or cardiologist tell you or a loved one that you only have a week to live, as was the case with me. They may not be aware of what is going on in the medical field – more on the LVAD and how it works later on.

MY STORY

First of all, who am I? No, I was not born on a hilltop in Tennessee, but in a Lake Superior border town of about 2,000 people in northern Wisconsin. I was born in my parents' house in1937. No hospital birth, but by gosh I made it into this world. Yes, I was sent to this world to be tested and I surely have been. I was not alone in our family. I have two older brothers and one older sister. Unfortunately, my father died at age thirty-five from Leukemia. Sadly the only thing I remember about my dad was that he broke a wooden paddle over my bottom when spanking me. I was an 8-year-old boy when my father died and left my mother with four children. My mother with only an 8th grade education and in a small town with little and limited employment opportunities had to struggle. At that time there was no social security, no Medicaid, no pension or life insurance from my deceased father, and no kind of government help.

Isn't it funny that now days so many people think the government should totally take care of them. They seem to lack a sense of responsibility and moral insight. How nice this country would be if we lived up to what President John F. Kennedy asked us to do in 1964. "Ask not what your country can do for you, but what you can do for your country."

But, okay, on with my story, my mother did find menial jobs such as bartending, grocery clerk (no union wages), and finally for her the big bonanza of being custodian in the local, public school district. The custodial job eventually gave her a lifelong pension, health insurance and a decent working wage that made her life much more agreeable.

My youth was one of loneliness in an unaffectionate home. I don't recall my mother ever saying she loved me. She rarely hugged me. Her message always to all of us was that if we misbehaved or got into any type of trouble she would send us to a state penitentiary for boys and girls at Green Bay, Wisconsin. We believed her as she showed little love for us. Part of the lack of love for us was rooted in the dislike she had for my father and his parents. She just didn't care. When my mother was home she did housework and had no time for us kids. My older siblings had their friends and I was the "Lone Ranger." For a few years I had a mongrel dog called Pepe. However, she became ill and died. It was a true loss for me!

Parents, grandparents love your children. Your love is worth more than any material things you may give them. Show your love by hugging, kissing, and telling your children in their earliest ages that you love them. Don't stop telling them just because they are growing older. We all need to know we are loved throughout our lives.

I started playing sports at an early age. I would play basketball and baseball day and night when I could. Of course, baseball in the spring and summer, but basketball I would practice year round. I was an outstanding basketball player and student up to the eighth grade. In the eighth grade I began to help a few other students in a tutoring session group outside of the classroom. I would give help mainly in math and spelling.

Back then in our school the eighth grade was a self-contained room with all subjects taught by the same teacher, except for music, which was taught by a woman teacher. She gave me the only "F" I ever received in grade school. She said I had a good voice and musical talent, but I was to belligerent, defiant, and uncooperative. At the time I thought she had the problem, not me. But that defiant attitude had probably developed within me from the lonely and impoverished life I led.

It really hurt to see happy families with a father and mother who seemed to love their children. It was tough also from the standpoint that in those days a widowed woman with four kids and a menial job were not the social choice of anyone. Even the Lutheran Church didn't want anything to do with us. I guess because my mother didn't give the church enough money. Not to associate with our family was the under lying social message. Oh, those were tough days. Cardboard in the shoes to protect the feet, no dental work, wearing the same clothes most of the time. And, rarely did we have enough to eat. My breakfast was always butter and peanut butter on toast dipped in coffee. We never had cereal, bacon, eggs, milk, etc. in the house.

During the summer between the seventh and eighth grade I had an interesting experience picking strawberries. In the early months of the summer a bus came to my hometown to pick up a number of young people who were interested in making money. We rode the bus to a town about ten miles away called Bayfield, Wisconsin. Bayfield is a lot like San Francisco. It is hilly yet the land blends down into the shores of Lake Superior. Bayfield is the central point for visitors who want to see the Apostle Islands National Park on Lake Superior. It is a small city of about twelve hundred population. Bayfield is a little city with great heart and character.

We picked strawberries for an older Swedish couple that had a massive strawberry field on the outer edge of Bayfield. The reason the strawberry picking stuck in my mind was the friendships I made there while getting away from my home, and making some desperately needed money. The Swedish owner always walked through the fields and implored us by saying "Hey, pick'em da berries and no play". It was always good to hear his accent. We always laughed, but it did keep us more focused on picking. The berry picking lasted for about four weeks. It was an interesting time, but it was hard work.

During my time in high school academics were far from my mind. I can honestly say that I never took any schoolwork home, so obviously I never did any homework. This explains my high school rank of being twenty-eighth of thirty-two students. In contrast, when I took the exam for a Masters degree I placed first of forty -four students. Desire and hard work can make a big difference. If I had received guidance and direction from someone whom I respected in high school, perhaps my academics might have been more of a priority. No teachers, coaches, clergy, etc. were interested in me as a person. Well, that's probably what made me become a public school guidance counselor.

My high school years were devoted to athletics (football, basketball and baseball) and to working nights at least three times a week from 7:00 P.M. to 11:00 P.M. My typical day from September through May was to attend school from 8:00 A.M. to approximately 3:30 P.M. After school I would spend two hours practicing one of the three major sports. At 6:00 P.M. I would go home to whatever I could find to eat (usually one or two cold hot dogs). Then I walked to the bowling alley to set pins from 7:00 P.M. to 11:00 P.M. Setting pins in those days was manually picking up the pins, putting them into the pin rack and lowering it to the floor to release the pins to their correct positions. It was dangerous work because the pins would fly in all directions when hit by the ball. Fortunately, in those days when the ladies bowled I could work two machines at a time. For the most part their bowling balls came down the lanes very slowly, so it was easy to handle two lanes at a time. After work I would go across the street to the local restaurant/arcade to have a hamburger and drink a soda. That was my routine for four years during the school week. Basketball games occupied two nights a week. On weekends I would work where I could find jobs.

My mother insisted that I go to church every Sunday even though the only time I ever went to church with her was at my father's funeral. But I made up for it after leaving my mother's house. I never attended church. I just didn't feel that the church or God were on my side until much, much, much later in life.

It was my ability and dedication to play basketball that provided me with opportunities. As a freshman in high school I started on the varsity team. I was probably the only ninth grader in my hometown to ever be a starter on the high school varsity team. I was the youngest in my class, only thirteen as a starting player. It wasn't long before the school and town began to recognize me for what I could do in sports. In my senior year I was the captain of the all conference team. In that school year (1954-55) I averaged 26.5 points a game. I usually sat out over a quarter of the game because of the tremendous leads we would have over the opposition. We played our final game of the season against a high school of twelve hundred students. This game would determine if we went to the state tournament or not. At that time there was only one state champion. It didn't matter if you were from a school of two thousand students or twenty-five, one champion only. I had 32 points in that game but we still lost. I was so tired in the last few minutes of the second half of that game that I could hardly jump. I know one time the opposing forward was going up for a rebound and to his surprise I had a hold of his shorts. He started to go up and his pants started down. He quit going for the rebound. Yes, I did let go of his pants.

My mother never once attended any of my high school or college games. If it hadn't been for sports I think I would have had a very difficult time in high school, as my only thoughts were to make money to buy clothes and food. Sports and the recognition it gave me kept me in school.

In my junior year I was chosen prom king, granted there weren't many to choose from in a class of thirty-two. However I did win the vote of my classmates. In order to attend that prom I had to get a driver's license so I would be able to drive my mother's boyfriend's car. In those days you went to the local police department and the chief of police would give you a behind the wheel test. The first time I had ever driven a car was when I took this manual-shift car to the police station for the driving test. The chief came out and we went for a drive. I could hardly shift the gears correctly. We stopped on a street that was uphill, the chief said to shut off the motor and start it up again. Well, I did, but the car must have rolled back some 12 feet before I got it going again. The chief said,

"That's OK. It just takes time to learn." He passed me and I got my license. Fortunately, I was in a small town, today I would never have gotten the license with the big government control. And, ironically, later in life I taught driver's education behind the wheel for the local public high school where I lived with my wife and three daughters.

Don Bellile
6' Jr. Forward
Figure 1

The girl I took to the prom was the prom queen. She must have thought I was a totally socially inept person. She would have been right in her thinking. It was bad enough that I could hardly drive the car. But to make it all worse, the car stopped when I was making a turnaround at a closed local restaurant/ nightclub. I had trouble getting it going again. The owners of the restaurant who lived above the club told me to get out or they would call the police. Fortunately, I got the car going and we got out of there. Not having much confidence in anything, I took the queen home. I bet she was really happy to be home. I wasn't much into dating in high school because that took money and I didn't have any. So, my social life wasn't all that great.

I think part of it was also because when I was young I somehow broke my nose. The septum was growing crooked, and I was really self-conscious about it. I approached my mother about it, who for once contacted a member of the county welfare department. The department approved money for me to go to the University Of Wisconsin Hospital in Madison to have my nose fixed. I was fifteen years old when I got on the Greyhound bus by myself and travelled three hundred sixty miles to have what I thought was a straightening of the septum. I stayed overnight at the YMCA and went to the hospital early the next day. What a scary experience for a young man from a small Northern Wisconsin town to go to the state capital and try to find housing and the hospital. I had very little money so it was tough. This was a side venture for me during the summer between my junior and senior years in high school. The doctors never did straighten my septum but they put some type of substance around it to take away the crooked look.

Another venture I had in high school was going to the old high school that had burned down some six years before I entered the new school. We had a coal-burning furnace we didn't always have coal and it gets very, very cold in northern

Wisconsin. I would go up to the ruins of the old high school and bring back home all the timber and other products that would burn. We had an axe so I was able to chop up the wood and materials. I don't feel it was stealing because everything was going to rot anyway. But, oh, I dreaded to be seen hauling the wood so I did all the carrying of wood, timbers, and other useful items at night. People knew we were in poverty, but how embarrassing it would have been to be seen in effect demonstrating our poverty.

One last happening in high school was that I also played football for three years. I was a starting guard on defense. I was, at the time, six feet one inch tall and weighed two hundred ten pounds. I was effective at the position. We had a good team in our junior year and probably would have been much better if I had played in my senior year. However, the doctors at the University Of Wisconsin Hospital had warned me that if I got a good hit on the nose I could bleed to death. Being apprehensive about that and the always ill fitting shoes, pads, and other equipment I decided to forego six or seven games and take my chances with basketball. The reason I added this story was because another player's father was standing near me during a home game. He commented, loud enough for me to hear, to another father some disparaging remarks about my not playing football. He continued to say I was letting the team down; His words really hurt my feelings. This is the same father who dropped fifty-cent pieces on the basketball floor when his son was shooting free throws. It was suppose to be an incentive to make the free throw. I guess the moral of this is whether you are young or old, think before you speak and be concerned about other people's feelings. It is not up to us to judge other people. The judge of other people is our Heavenly Father.

After high school graduation I could not get a "real" job because I was still only 17 years old. Therefore, that summer I was the city lifeguard at the local Lake Superior beach. Let me tell you that water in Lake Superior is so cold most of the time that you could keep soft drinks nice and cool in there. Nobody asked me if I could swim, but fortunately I could swim reasonably well. Nothing eventful happened that summer. In the fall of 1955 I attended the University of Wisconsin – Superior campus on a leadership scholarship from basketball. I started school with thirty-five dollars and a number of cans of soup that my mother had given my brother and me. My brother was attending college for the first time in his life too. He had recently returned home from a two- year stint with the United States Army in Germany.

Until basketball started I would work at my hometown-casting foundry on weekends. I would ride back and forth to Superior with my brother. After one semester my brother quit attending school. I began hitchhiking the sixty-five miles to my hometown. That is when I was not playing basketball on the weekends. In those days you could hitchhike and be safe. Not true now with all the perverts there are in our society. My brother and I had rented a room in a private home near the college. It had radiator hot heat and that is how we warmed up our soup. Along with soup, crackers, bread, peanut butter and other inexpensive foods we would sustain ourselves. As far as the basketball went I made the starting five on the varsity team. I had a good year athletically, but not academically. Socially, it didn't happen. It was a tough year and when basketball season was over I got a night job at the Chung King Noodle Factory in Duluth, Minnesota. Duluth is across the bridge from Superior, Wisconsin. I shoveled noodles four to five hours a night. Man! That was something else!

I think now days of the whining and crying of high school graduates who want to go to college. They cry, cry, cry. They don't have enough money for tuition, books, housing, social life, cell phones, and oh yes, a car! Maybe when they leave high school they ought to work for a year or two. Maybe they should go to a junior college, or do online classes and forget about the big cost private schools and some of the meaningless educations they provide. Does it hurt to have a part time job while attending school? No, I don't think so. But, you might have to give up some social life and vacations in Cancun or wherever. Gee, maybe the students would have to sacrifice a little, and gosh they might even have to use public transportation.

Well, again, that's not what this book is about, but I get so irritated when we have children in this country without food and healthcare, and the government keeps handing out money for post high school education. It's a joke, but a sad one. Only about 38% of public high school students in general should be attending a traditional four-year college. The rest should be in trade schools. Let the federal government require a year or two of military service from these male and female students who would qualify for a trade school, college, etc. They would get a grant based on their contribution to the military. Well, enough said.

After that first year of college, I needed a job for the summer and at last I was now 18 years old. Unfortunately, the whole economy was on hold because of the steel strike. So what was I to do? Stay with my mother and be a hermit without much food and no money? Nope, I decided to go from one ship to the next that were docked at the Duluth and Superior shipyards. Because of the strike there was no need for the ships to carry iron ore or grain but I did go from ship to ship until I was hired as a coal passer to the fireman on the ship. Again the ship wasn't running so I was given odd jobs until the strike was over. When the strike ended that summer I decided that I would stay on the ship until the end of the shipping season in later November. Sailing on the Great Lakes was quite an experience. One time in August on Lake Michigan we had such a tremendous storm that we only made a half-mile forward in a 24-hour period. On another occasion we ran into another ship on the Chicago River, but our speed was so slow that there was hardly any damage. The boat was laid up in December of that year. The boating season was at an end.

It was time to start school again. I had saved the money that I made for college. However, there were a couple of other things I needed to purchase. I used some of the money to pay my mother's coal bill and some other expenses. I purchased a 1951 Ford sedan and started back to college at Superior in January of 1957.

Missing the first semester was hard on me. I didn't do as well in basketball as I did in my freshman year. The course of studies I took was not of much interest to me and it wasn't long before my money ran out. The basketball coach did not help out much with the situation. I was in a no food, no money, and losing interest (burning out) in the basketball situation. So, I decided that the following year I would attend a private college about 18 miles from my hometown, that way I could drive and commute with other students on a daily basis. I didn't have to pay rent and my mother would feed me.

When the school year was over I went back to work as a night cook on the same ore boat as I had worked on as a coal passer. This time I got the night cook job. It was interesting and fun to do, except for a third engineer on the boat. He always wanted his eggs to be poached for a certain time, and if it didn't come out right he would have a fit. Other than him, the rest of the crew was very good. I decided to stay on as a cook until the ship laid up in December. I would have enough money saved up by that time to last for the second semester of college and beyond.

The private college I attended the second semester provided me with tuition and books. I played on the varsity basketball team that semester and the following year.

Between my junior and senior years in college I worked for an explosives company. The pay was good and I would be sitting pretty well for my senior year, I thought. By this time I had really "burned out" on basketball.

Instead of playing basketball in my senior year I worked at night at a plywood veneer factory in the city where the college was located. I concentrated more on my schoolwork than ever before. Of course at the end of my senior year I graduated with a Bachelor's degree in Biology and minors in History and Physical Education.

After graduation I received a teaching and coaching position in a small northern Wisconsin town for the magnificent sum of forty-two hundred dollars a year. I taught high school biology and the boys' and girls' physical education. I also was the head basketball coach and track and field coach. I stayed in a private house. The sleeping room was adequate, but there was no refrigerator or anything. So, I had to eat at the very few restaurants in town. What a dog's life.

I was twenty-one years old and my students were from fourteen to nineteen years old. The high school took in a large geographical area around the town. There were a number of poor whites and Native Americans that attended the school. Some of the Native American students had dirt floors in their houses. The whole year was a challenge. I did gain experience in teaching and was offered a contract for the following year with a two hundred dollar raise. Wow! Was that impressive, huh?

Fortunately, a friend had applied for a teaching job in the state of Alaska with the On Base School System for the military. He got the job and was going to start at sixty-four hundred dollars a year. I thought, "Hey that may be a worthwhile experience". So, I applied and was offered an elementary position teaching physical education. I accepted the job. That August my friend and I left for Anchorage, Alaska where we had teaching jobs on Elmendorf Air Force Base. The on-base schools at the time were run by the state of Alaska and the pay came from the state as well. I taught physical education to first grade through seventh grade. Actually, for most of the year I taught a half-day as the military taught swimming at the military field house. I chaperoned the students over and back and kept a watch on them while swimming. An uneventful year, but I met a lot of special teachers who were really dedicated to their jobs. Social life wasn't much, just drank alcohol and smoked a lot. I did do a little hunting and fishing.

After that first year of teaching my friend and I went back home to Wisconsin for the summer. Once again I was almost broke. So my friend and I got jobs at a foundry outside of Milwaukee, Wisconsin in a city called Waukesha. That job was perhaps the dirtiest job I have ever had.

In August we left again for another teaching year in Anchorage. It was more of the same as far as the job went. However, I took a three-credit course in German through the University of Alaska with another friend that I met while teaching. We were going to go to Germany the following summer, the trip never happened. My friend was transferred to teach in another city in Alaska. He was an avid fisherman, but died at a young age when his boat tipped over and his fishing boots filled up with water. He was a great friend and a great teacher.

That summer my friend from my hometown and I got summer jobs with the Alaska Department of Fish and Game. Our jobs were to stop commercial fishermen from netting salmon in fresh water areas where they had gone to spawn. We were armed with a 38 pistol and a rifle. The Fish and Game would drop us off either by pontoon plane or by boat. All of this law enforcement we did took place in the Alaska Peninsula. We would setup camp out of sight and watch for the illegal fishing boats. We made two arrests that summer and saved thousands of dollars for the state, not to mention the propagation of fish.

One arrest was in the early morning of a regular weekday. The fishermen started netting and I got into our kayak and started out for the boat. I was paddling with one hand and the other held the pistol. The fishermen were so busy they didn't see me coming. I had gotten real close to the boat when my kayak tipped over and dumped me out. Fortunately, the water was about waist high. I stood there and announced that I was a "law enforcement officer" with the Fish & Game department and that they were under arrest. I told them that my partner was on shore with a rifle aimed at them. I looked at the shoreline and my partner was nowhere to be seen, however, in a few minutes he appeared. At the trial I found out that one of the fishermen was from the state of Washington and had a criminal record for manslaughter. Our other arrest was of Native Alaskans. They got out of the charge of illegal fishing because of a hung jury.

While we were in the Alaska Peninsula we discovered what we thought was copper in some of the rock formations. We decided to go back the following summer with dynamite to check it out. Let's get into my third year of teaching in Alaska.

The difference in my third year of teaching was that I started to get friendly with a female teacher on base. We started to date quite a bit and liked each other quite well. When summer came she went back to her hometown in the state of Idaho.

Meanwhile, I stayed in Anchorage and worked as a switchman on the Alaska Railroad. At that time the federal government operated the train. I remember trips where we would go by a local golf course. If the engineer saw any golf balls he would stop the train to pick them up. On the trips toward Fairbanks we would make stops to drop-off and pick-up fishermen on the way. The fishermen would ride the train. They asked the engineer to stop the train to let them off at isolated areas to do recreational fishing. When they were finished with their fishing they would walk back to the tracks to wait for the next train going in the direction they wanted. The train would stop to pick them up. After a month or so I decided to quit the railroad and go back to Wisconsin for a while, before returning to Anchorage.

A few weeks before school was to begin my girlfriend from Idaho drove to my hometown to meet my family. After seeing the sights in my home area we traveled back to Anchorage together.

During my third year of teaching Anchorage had the largest earthquake in its history; it registered about 8.2 on the Richter scale. I had never experienced an earthquake before, so living on an airbase at the time I thought we were being bombed. There was extreme damage and loss of lives from the quake. I never did get use to the many tremors that followed the big quake. Other than the earthquake, my third year of teaching went well for me. My girlfriend and I spent a lot of time together.

In the summer following that third year my Wisconsin friend and I loaded up a pontoon plane with dynamite and flew back to the Alaska Peninsula to do a little prospecting for copper, silver, or whatever. The weather that summer was cool in the peninsula but we stayed there for about a week. We were exploding dynamite sticks all over the area. We had a good time and staked out some ore claims and had them recorded in Anchorage. These claims did not amount to anything. The location of the claims being that far out on the Peninsula made it too expensive to mine and transport the ore to processing facilities. But, we did have some nice copper samples.

My fourth and final year in Alaska was noteworthy because I got married in October of 1964 to my girlfriend from Idaho. After we got married it wasn't long before the responsibilities of marriage hit me and I developed a good case of shingles. If you haven't had shingles consider yourself quite lucky. Mine wasn't severe and didn't last long but it was painful. I have never had a case of reoccurrence since that time in 1964. I guess I made the adjustment if shingles is related to stress. My wife and I are still married today and will be celebrating our 46th wedding anniversary in October 2010.

After marriage my wife continued teaching for the rest of the school year. A baby girl was born prematurely by a number of months and died after a few days. Today that baby probably would have made it with today's advanced hospital techniques. My wife and I decided that year that Alaska was not, in our opinion, the best place to raise a family in future years. The weather most of the year is cold, wet and the winter darkness is depressing. We left Anchorage that summer for Madison, Wisconsin where I was going to see about law school admission at the University of Wisconsin. However, the day we arrived at the university it was packed with war protestors, hippies, and what have you. It was complete turmoil. I looked at my wife and said, "Let's go to Milwaukee and look for teaching positions".

Once in the Milwaukee area we decided to apply for teaching positions in the suburban school districts. My wife ended up teaching first grade in a suburban public school while I obtained a physical education position in a different suburban school district. It certainly was a big change from Alaska back to Wisconsin. The Milwaukee area was a great area to teach and to live. Milwaukee and the surrounding suburbs were a wonderful place to raise our family.

We bought our first dog, a beautiful white female toy poodle. We called her Mitzi. She was a joy to us for twelve years. After Mitzi died we bought another white female toy poodle and called her Candy. Candy was a wonderful dog and she lived for eighteen years. We now have an apricot colored female toy poodle and she is presently twelve years old. All three dogs certainly had different personalities. One thing that was true of all three; their love for us and how much they liked to be loved. A toy poodle is, at least to my knowledge, the second smallest of poodles. Our three dogs averaged about five to ten pounds in weight and were about nine inches tall and about seventeen inches in length from top of head to tail.

It was in our third year of teaching in Wisconsin that we adopted our beautiful baby girl whom we named Karlyn.

Today Karlyn is now thirty-nine years old and has five beautiful children and a great husband. Later on we had two other girls whom we named Allison and Danielle. My wife had difficulty carrying pregnancies to term. She had to spend all of her pregnancy time in bed or on a couch.

Allison graduated from Utah State University and today is an Account Manager in Salt Lake City, Utah. She owns her own home and is a delight in our life. She is intelligent, pretty, charitable, and has a great sense of humor. We are still hoping she will meet the right man, get married, and have children. What a prize she would be for some guy.

Our daughter Danielle also graduated from Utah State University in Logan, Utah. She received a degree in business information systems. She now has three wonderful little boys and who knows how many are forthcoming. She married a Utah State graduate and they purchased his father's dairy farm. My wife and I are fortunate to have three great daughters and two wonderful sons-in-law. And of course, we are certainly blessed with eight grandchildren whom we love dearly.

I taught school for thirty-three years before I took disability for two years because of my bad heart situation. For most of those years I was either a middle school or high school Guidance Counselor. I finished my career at the high school level. I did enjoy nine years as a physical education and biology teacher.

College is not for everyone, as I have previously mentioned. I don't know why so many students and parents are so adverse to a one or two year trade school. Today a lot of those students who choose trade school are working while the four-year college graduates with a degree are not working. A lot of my students had difficulties making it through high school. Yet, bless their hearts, they would always talk about going to college. Our President even talks about college for all. How unrealistic and frustrating for at least 65% of our students in a "normal" school district. Parents do their children a disservice when all they talk about is a college degree.

Also, get real, America teachers are vastly underpaid and high quality leaders do not administer schools. Most of the administration positions are not filled by people with ability or leadership qualities but by persons who will follow the line with the top administration. The federal government has to give public school teachers a tax credit to improve upon their lives. Like happy cows make for better milk, happy teachers and happy students make for happier and better learning students. The federal government has to stop throwing all the billions of dollars at education with no viable results. Most of the federal money doesn't help students, but pads the pockets of newly or existing "directors", worthless equipment and materials, and just "lost" monies.

The answer to the education crisis (in my opinion) is tax credits for a nationwide mentor-tutor system. We need to utilize parents, singles, and others who have the time to work from ten too fifteen hours (or more) per week with two or three students at a time. These mentors, under the direction of the classroom teacher, would work on whatever skills the students need to improve upon. What these students need are not only help with the academic work, but also with life skills. We need caring, well-balanced human beings who can help students with their self-concept. This mentor program could easily be done with good administrative leadership in individual schools and leadership from the superintendent along with his or her staff. Of course, local school boards would have to provide the encouragement to all school personnel. Mentors would have to go through a strong screening and security check. Mentors would receive tax credits equal to perhaps about nine dollars an hour. A by-product of the mentoring program would be the opening up of thousands or millions of other jobs in society. This would happen because qualifying mentors would give up present jobs that pay $15,000 to $24,000 to do the mentoring. There are many mothers, fathers, and others who would rather be working in a school near their homes. This could result in parents spending more time with their own children and doing society a great service, while benefiting their own financial situation. A program like this could improve the quality of life for not only the mentors, but for teachers, parents, school students, and society in general. It would save the federal government billions of dollars. This mentor plan would also save the state governments millions of dollars. It is a win-win situation for everyone. This plan would be for elementary, middle, and high school students. We would have no need for so called "Charter" schools, which in most cases are in education just to make money. For every good Charter school there are ten others that are not doing the job of educating youth, but are concerned about their profits. The mentor plan would be great for inner city schools. It could reduce dropout rates, immediately. It would also reduce crime and drugs because young people would feel they are of worth. Schools without failure could be realized with this plan. Two good states to try this mentor plan are Utah and Illinois. Utah would be a good state because of the many family orientated LDS members who would rather be with their families and doing charitable work. Illinois would be good because of the inner schools of Chicago, as well as other large cities in the state that have a diversity of background. I have many ideas on education but that is not what this book is all about.

What this book is really about is providing knowledge, hope, and extended life to millions of people in the United States and throughout the world who are dying from congestive heart failure. It is about lives that could be saved, like mine, with the medical knowledge and devices that are available today. Many general practitioners and even cardiologists are not even aware of the knowledge or options that are available for their patients. Their attitude is if the pills don't fix it then forget it and here's the name of a hospice. This is what my general practitioner told my wife two and a half ago. He said I had a week to live. I got out of that local hospital and went to San Diego where I was on the Heart Transplant List. The doctors there installed a heart pump. More about the heart pump lifesaver later.

In the early years of life I always thought I had a heart problem. Even though I played athletics, I was always sort of pinkish skinned when I was exercising at a high peak. No other athletes seemed to look "flushed" that way. I did go in for yearly athletic physicals in high school in order to participate in athletics. However, the exam for athletes was a check for a hernia and an eyeball look at you. I really can't remember having my blood pressure or my heart beat checked.

I was about thirty-two when my wife and I were driving back to Milwaukee after a visit with my sister and her family that I had a violent pain in my chest. This event lasted for about two minutes, I thought maybe I had eaten too much or was smoking too much. Anyway, it subsided and I forgot about it.

About eight years later at the age of forty I had a massive heart attack that destroyed the tissue on the right side of my heart, this happened shortly after our youngest daughter was born. The doctors after doing a heart catherization told me that I had several smaller heart attacks in the past. I thought about it and recalled what must have been another heart attack when I was traveling to Montana to attend graduate school at Montana State University. I didn't recognize it as an attack, but the intense chest pain now suggests to me that it was. Of course, I just blamed the pain on the traveling and chain smoking I did at the time. I used to smoke two to three packs of cigarettes a day. I haven't smoked now for more than thirty years. Yes, smoking probably helped contribute to my heart problems, however, in doing genealogy research I found that most of all the Bellile men died in their late fifties to mid sixties from heart disease. One exception to that heart history my own father who died of leukemia when he was thirty-five years old. You can't abuse your body even if the genetics are in your favor.

I have a brother-in-law who has weighed more than 340 pounds for most of his life. He is now seventy years old and has never had heart disease. My wife (his sister) had a heart catherization about ten years ago and the cardiologist related to her that her arteries were as clean as a newborn baby. I won't tell you her weight right now, but she is about sixty-five pounds over what she should be. Neither my wife nor her brother has ever smoked. They have had no ancestry with heart problems. The message here, checkout your family history and perhaps do some preventive maintenance on your body.

Smoking certainly has a damaging effect on your overall health. When I started smoking in the 1950's it was considered "cool". It is not "cool" today or ever. Incidentally, when I was in college, a starter on the basketball team and financially destitute, the basketball coach directed a representative of the Leggett and Meyers Tobacco Company to me. The representative wanted a college person to distribute free packs of cigarettes to students. I had to learn a little speech about cigarettes and, of course, smoke them. In return for my services the company gave me some cartons of cigarettes.

It was 17 years later, after the episode of the massive tissue destroying heart attack at forty, that I ended up back in the hospital for open heart surgery, the actual surgery went well. The surgeons replaced six heart arteries with veins from my right leg and chest. However, things did not go well with my recovery. I had a heart arrhythmia that I still have today. The skipping of beats warranted a heart pacer which I have had replaced about three times now. Electro-physiologists tried on three different occasions to find the source of the irregularity, but they couldn't find it. It usually takes about five days after open-heart surgery and you go home. So many things went wrong with me that I was a patient for a month and a half. My kidneys shut down, I became a real number two diabetic, and I would have large accumulations of body fluid. Finally, after seventy-five days and feeling somewhat better, I begged the cardiologist to let me go home. He did let me go home, but he wasn't very positive about it. I swear, as this hospital was a teaching facility for doctors, they were keeping me there for the final exam for the students. After I was released from the hospital I returned in two weeks with pneumonia. After getting the pneumonia taken care of I seemed to get much better. However, I did not have much energy and couldn't function well anymore. I applied for disability with my cardiologist's recommendation and I received it – ending my thirty-three year education career. My wife was still teaching and had about five more years to teach before she could qualify for early retirement. She didn't start back to teaching until all of our three children were in school.

At this time I had been on the heart transplant list for a few years. What a pain that was being on the heart transplant list! The heart transplant medical personnel required me to take tests after tests every year to stay on the list. I went year after year and received no heart transplant. After eight years I was on the top of the waiting list, but if you are walking and talking you still are not a priority. Those who are in the hospital and can't function outside of the hospital become the priorities for transplants. That constant emergency patient always seemed to be a step ahead of me. My blood type O positive did not help my case in getting a transplant either.

Finally my wife retired and one winter we went to visit her brother for a couple of weeks in Yuma, Arizona. Her brother is from Idaho and goes to Yuma every year during the winter months. Yuma has fantastic weather in the winter. Nearly every day is sunny and cloudless with a temperature somewhere between the low 60's and high 70's. It rarely rains. There are citrus trees (I have six in my yard), lettuce, cabbage, melons, broccoli, and many other vegetables that are grown there. Yuma is the lettuce capital of the United States. If you have arthritis this is the climate for you. We enjoyed our visit to Yuma so much that we bought a fourteen-foot wide trailer home in a 55+ park. We then began to spend the months from October through May in Yuma, and the rest of the year in Wisconsin.

After about four years as "winter visitors" in Yuma we decided we may as well quit worrying about what could happen to the house in Wisconsin while we were away living in Arizona. So we purchased a new modular house and had it placed on a lot we purchased in a 55+ subdivision across from a beautiful municipal golf course. It was a very wise move. Today we are still in the same house that has about 1,500 square feet. We have, as I previously mentioned, planted all types of citrus trees that are now producing quite nicely. I also have a nice raised garden area.

Living in Yuma made it necessary to transfer to the transplant list at the University of California – San Diego that is a three-hour drive from Yuma. I had been on the heart transplant list for seven months out of the year at UCSD and five months out of the year at St. Luke's Hospital in Milwaukee, Wisconsin prior to moving to Yuma year round. About three years later the UCSD Heart Transplant Clinic doctor informed me that because they did not do enough heart transplants they would no longer be a hospital for performing heart transplants. The doctors and medical personnel at UCSD were great, but it was out of their hands. They gave me the name of a cardiologist to contact at Sharp Hospital in San Diego. The medical personnel at Sharp along with the endorsement of UCSD concluded that I qualified to be on their transplant list. Once again, I started having the same hospital tests on a regular basis. And, of course, I was seeing the cardiologist on a monthly basis. As par for the course no hearts became available to me.

In the meantime I found out my blood platelet level had dropped to twenty-six. The normal range for the average person is from one hundred-thirty to four hundred. The consequence of such a low level was that I could start bleeding and possibly bleed to death. My cardiologist lined me up with a hematologist. He started me on an intense drug therapy program. The chemotherapy was intended to raise my platelet level. While the therapy made me fall and feel terrible it did raise my platelet level to about 75. After the treatment my body began to fill up with fluids and I had problems breathing, walking, and sleeping. I ended up in the local hospital where they took many pounds of fluid out of me. My local doctor told my wife he knew of a good hospice and thought I would be dead in about a week. This was in October of 2007. Today it is May of 2010. I am obviously alive and doing well. The reason I am not dead is because my wife and I got out of the Yuma hospital and rushed to San Diego.

THE LVAD

We met with my cardiologist and he presented the information about the left ventricular assist device (LVAD). He sent me over to a heart surgeon who discussed the LVAD-XVE and the HeartMate II pumps. He reviewed all of my heart test data and concluded that I would probably be able to survive the implantation of the LVAD-XVE pump. But, he was quite hesitant about doing the surgery because of my low platelet level and the possibility of bleeding to death on the operating table. After a long talk and discussing the alternative to surgery (death) he agreed to put in the pump, LVAD-XVE. That pump would cause the least amount of bleeding. The pump was put in during the latter part of November of 2007. I was not fit enough to leave the hospital until January 3, 2008. Once released the hospital wanted us to stay in a local motel for a week. A visiting nurse came in every day to check my vitals and help with my adjustment outside of the hospital environment.

Everything went well that week except the vision in one eye became blurred. We found an ophthalmologist and had the eye examined. No detached retina, which was the first thing, the doctor worried about. Eventually, and after a shot in my eyeball, the eye healed and returned to normalcy.

After the motel stay we went back to Yuma to recuperate. It was interesting that after the surgery the surgeon indicated that I didn't bleed much at all during the surgery. The following months went by fast. I had a home care nurse visit once a week to check my vitals. I recuperated nicely. We went about our life as normal. We even did some traveling.

It wasn't until September of 2008 that I started hearing a clinking sound from my pump. I thought, gosh, it's only been a little over eight months since the pump was installed. Surely, I thought, it can't be going out on me. So, we called the LVAD coordinators at Sharp Hospital. They told us to come over there immediately, which we did. The coordinator took out a dirty air filter and replaced it with a new one. They sent the old filter to Boston to have it analyzed to see if minerals from the pump were present in the filter. If there were minerals present, it was the pump self-destructing. We went back to Yuma. Two days later we got a recorded message saying a date for my next open heart surgery had been set. This made two open-heart surgeries in less than a year. They removed the old pump that was ready to stop functioning.

A better pump called the HeartMate II LVAD was installed. The first pump I had was suppose to last up to three years, but I only got about nine months use out of it. Again, the reason they put the LVAD-XVE pump in was because of the great potential for bleeding associated with the HeartMate LVAD II. The new LVAD II is now being tested worldwide. I am one of six hundred forty-eight patients in the experimental group.

You are probably wondering if I am still on the heart transplant list. No, I am not. The hospital took me off the list after being on it for ten years because of my blood problems, diabetes, and age. I no longer qualified for a transplant. That organ transplant situation is a tough one. When I was reasonably healthy and could have withstood the surgery no hearts (at least to me) were available. Then as I got older and when some of these other afflictions came up they said I no longer qualified for a transplant. It is fortunate that a lot of young people sign their driver's license to donate their organs, but when the time comes I think it is unfortunate that parents object to it. What a waste of body organs. I guess what motivates most people is money. So, there has to be some type of financial remuneration in order to expedite organ donations. Well, that's the way it goes I guess.

Wow! The surgery for the second pump took about twelve hours by a team of doctors. The doctors had to take out the old pump and cord that went through my chest to the outside of the body that connects to the controller and power pack (batteries). They had to find and create a new pouch for the new pump. I came into the second surgery in much better condition than when I received the first pump. As a result, I was out of the hospital in thirteen days. Once I got home I started getting my strength back again and things went well until my wife and I visited our daughters in Salt Lake City, Utah. It was at the end of the summer of 2008 just before we were scheduled to fly back to Yuma, Arizona. I passed out walking up the driveway of my youngest daughter's house. Feeling better the next day we flew home to Yuma. I continued to get weaker each of the next two days. Into the Emergency

Room we went. After some blood tests it was determined I was bleeding internally.

Subsequently, I ended up in Sharp Hospital after taking a flight for life helicopter ride from Yuma to San Diego. The doctors concluded after many tests that I was bleeding from the small intestine, but because the small intestine is quite long they were unable to locate the specific point of the bleeding. The doctors stopped the drug Coumadin that I had been taking. Coumadin is a blood thinner that aids in preventing the formation of blood clots. They also placed me on liquid diet for thirteen days. Finally, after the thirteen days the bleeding stopped. I was released to go home.

I don't know what caused the vessel to bleed and really neither did the doctors. What was funny about the situation was the doctors' digestive group didn't think Medicare and my secondary insurance were paying them enough for their "expert services". Talk about greed, it really is magnified in healthcare. I think throughout the years that I have been seeing doctors only about 35% of them really cared about me as a patient. The rest were in the medical field for the money only. I was blessed to have great heart doctors in San Diego who really cared about my health and me as a person. And, I can say the nurses at Sharp Hospital were also excellent, caring people.

Now let's take a look at the HeartMate II LVAD. What it is, how does it work, who needs it, and where you can go to see if you qualify for HeartMate II? Now please be advised that I was a high school guidance counselor, driving instructor, and in order to support my family, a part-time residential real estate salesman. I am not a doctor. I gleaned the following information from all my readings and personal experience. Technical information and pictures that are in this book have been provided through the courtesy of Thoratec Corporation in allowing me to reproduce it. Thoratec is the manufacturer of the HeartMate II LVAD. Before we start with information on the LVAD, let's look at congestive heart failure.

Congestive heart failure (CHF) means your heart isn't pumping enough blood to take care of your body properly and help it to function accurately. The term congestive heart failure (CHF) comes from blood backing up into the body organs. Prior to receiving the LVAD I had long-term heart failure. Some of the symptoms were fatigue and weakness, shortage of breath, reduced physical activity, and fluid retention. There are more symptoms, but I think these will suffice. In regard to fluid retention, I had twenty-four pounds of fluid removed from my body tissue prior to being taken into surgery to receive my first LVAD. As with many cases of heart failure my left ventricle, the main blood-pumping chamber of the heart, was not doing its job. Medicines, (I think I used every type of medicine possible to help heart failure), were not helping to improve my heart situation. I was taking large doses of water releasing pills but was still retaining fluid and gaining weight. My ejection fraction was about 12% and in a normal, healthy heart it would be about 60%. This means that 60% of the blood that fills the ventricle is pumped out with each heartbeat. This ejection factor indicates how well your heart is pumping and is used to classify heart failure and what treatment is to be provided. Another influence to my heart problem was the fact that I am a Type 2 diabetic.

Diabetes is a major cause of heart attacks, kidney disease, vision loss, peripheral artery disease, leg amputations, and nerve damage. Diabetes shortens life expectancy by about thirteen years, taking about 300,000 American lives annually. And, diabetes drains the United States' economy of more than 130 billion dollars a year, consuming about one in four Medicare dollars. Get an AIC test to see where you are with your blood glucose level. Diabetes can be controlled. Do it today. There are other diseases of course that affect the heart, but the big "D" is the toughest one.

What is the LVAD and how it works?

The Thoratec HeartMate II Left Ventricular Assist Device (LVAD) is a mechanical circulatory support (MCS) device intended for a broad range of advanced-stage heart failure patients. HeartMate II is designed to restore blood flow, improve survival, functional status, and quality of life.

The HeartMate II incorporates many features specifically intended to minimize the risk of complications and improve device durability while enhancing patient outcomes.

- Survival. The HeartMate II was designed with the objective of providing up to ten years of circulatory support for a broad range of advanced-stage heart failure patients.
- Quality of Life. The HeartMate II is an implantable device that facilitates freedom of movement, routine daily activities, travel and even some sports like golf- leading to an improved quality of life for patients.
- Home Discharge. HeartMate II patients can be discharged from the hospital, providing significant psychological and social benefits to the patient as well as cost savings to the patient and hospital alike.
- Simplicity/Ease-of-Use. The simple design – with one moving part – contributes substantially to reliable operation.
- Durability. The device's hydrodynamic bearings are designed to provide up to 10 years of support.

The HeartMate II is implanted alongside a patient's native heart and designed to take over the pumping ability of the weakened heart's left ventricle, which is responsible for pumping oxygen-rich blood from the diaphragm in the abdomen. It is attached to the aorta (the main artery that feeds blood into the entire body) from the natural heart, leaving natural circulation in place while providing all of the energy necessary to propel blood throughout the body. An external, wearable system that includes a controller and batteries is attached via an external driveline. A power cable connects the device to a small monitor, a power base unit.

The HeartMate II LVAS can pump up to 10 liters of blood per minute, covering the full output of a healthy heart. The HeartMate II is designed to provide long-term cardiac support for patients who have advanced-stage heart failure. An axial flow device, the HeartMate II is designed to have a much longer functional life than the previous generation of devices and to operate more simply and quietly. It is also smaller and designed to be easier to implant. Bench studies project that the HeartMate II LVAS has the capability to operate for up to ten years.

*Reprinted with permission from Thoratec Corporation.

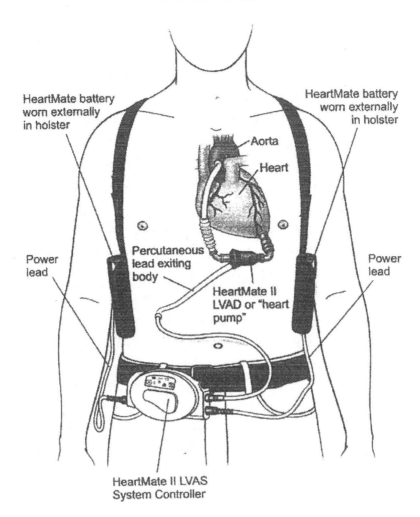

LVAD Heart Pump
Figure 2

As shown in **Figure 2,** a percutaneous lead passes through your skin. The outside of the lead is covered with a special material that lets skin cells grow into it. This helps the exit site heal. A well-healed exit site can lower the risk of infection.

Note: "Percutaneous" means "through the skin."

Power leads connect the System Controller to a power source (batteries, PBU or EPP). When the System Controller is connected to battery power, you'll wear 2 batteries, either in "holster" under the arms (**Figure 2**) or in a Carrying Case around your waist. The System Controller can also be powered by the Power Base Unit (PBU) that is plugged into a wall outlet (**Figure 3**).

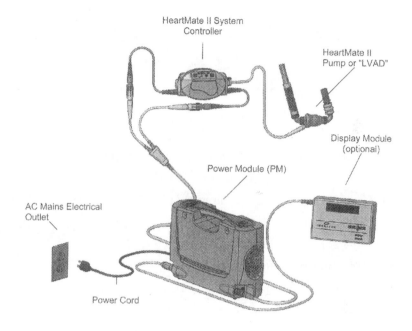

LVAD System
Figure 3

*Reprinted with permission from Thoratec Corporation
The HeartMate Power Module (PM) (**Figure 4**) is designed to:

- Provide to the HeartMate II LVAS during tethered operation (when connected to AC mains electrical power).
- Provide power to the Display Module when the optional Display Module is in use.
- Echo System Controller alarms.

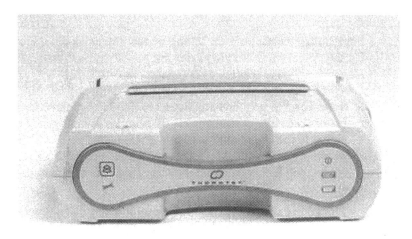

The Power Module (PM)
Figure 4

*Reprinted with permission form Thoratec Corporation.

The Universal Battery Charger **(Figure 5)** is compact and lightweight with rapid charging technology to complement an on-the-go lifestyle.
- Weighs only eight pounds-highly portable
- Rapid charging-4 hours
- Automatic discharge notification delivers consistent battery performance
- Intuitive light indicators provide readily-accessible battery status

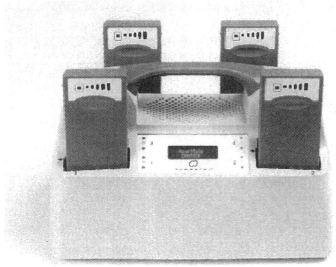

Battery Charger
Figure 5

*Reprinted with permission from Thoratec Corporation

The System Controller is a small computer that makes sure your pump is working properly. It is connected to both the pump and a power supply (batteries, PM, or EPP). The System Controller is usually worn on the belt or waistband.

The System Controller warns you if there is a problem with your pump or its power supply. The System Controller's warning lights, buttons, and battery fuel gauge are on the top of the Controller (**Figure 6**).

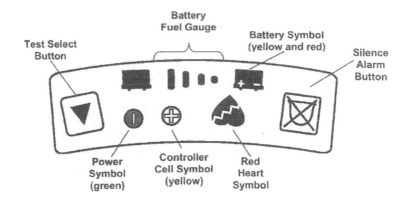

The System Controller
Figure 6

*Reprinted with permission from Thoratec Corporation

Probably some questions you might have now are about the quality of life with LVAD II. Let me reassure you that it is such a relief from where I was health wise. Prior to having the pump placed within me. The LVAD II was designed to help patients stay active. Activities such as sleeping (but not on the stomach), eating, intimacy, and car travel are the same as they are for regular, healthy people. However, car airbags could cause bleeding if an airbag hits your abdomen or chest. Some LVAD patients may have had the airbags eliminated in their cars. You can travel internationally; however, you need to find out if adapters or converters are needed for using electrical power in some foreign countries. It is also possible to shower with a special kit Thoratec provides to its patients.

Let me share personal experiences I have had with my battery holsters showing. Both experiences happened at church. People have asked if I am a F.B.I. agent or some type of special police officer. One young marine in our church first thought that I was a marine officer. He told me the officers in Iraq wore holsters (only with pistols in them) like mine.

I get lots and lots of looks when I am shopping or doing other things out in public. When physician assistants, general practitioners, and many cardiologists are not even aware of the LVAD's availability it is certainly understandable that I look a little strange to the average person.

What do LVAD patients say regarding the pump and quality of life? Names have been withheld. *

"I have a good life right now and the 'HeartMate' keeps me there, keeps me going, keeps me happy."

"I've been able to do everything and more than what I expected to be able to do, other than I can't swim in the pool."

"My doctor knew nothing about it, even my cardiologist didn't know about it and they're both ecstatic and wanting to learn, and now they know that there's hope for their patients."

"If I were talking to somebody who was trying to make the decision whether or not to get a heart pump I would definitely say to go ahead and do it."

"I've had an LVAD now for six years, and six years ago, you know, they did not give me a chance."

"I can get up in the morning, ride my bicycle, I can rake the leaves, and mow the lawn. I have no problems going up and down stairs."

*Reprinted with permission from the Thoratec Corporation.

Based in Pleasanton, California, Thoratec Corporation (Nasdaq: THOR) is a world leader in device based mechanical circulatory support therapies to save, support, and restore failing hearts. Thoratec in a recent press release said it received approval from the FDA at the end of 2008 to end randomization in its Destination Therapy (DT) pivotal clinical trial for the HeartMate II. In early December 2008, the company announced that a pre-specified interim analysis of data from the trial showed that patients implanted with the HeartMate II achieved statistically superior outcomes versus those in the control group who were implanted with the company's HeartMate XVE. This is the pump I first had placed into me. It was noisy and wore out for me in nine months. As a result, the study's Data Safety Monitoring Board concurred with Thoratec's plan to eliminate randomization for all the additional patients enrolled in the DT study under FDA-authorized Continued Access Protocols. The company plans to file its PreMarket Approval (PMA) seeking FDA approval of the HeartMate II for DT in late May of 2009 leading to an expected approval in the first half of 2010. As of January 23, 2009, there were 648 patients enrolled in the DT arm of trial and I am one of those 648 patients.

I am so impressed with Thoratec that I have purchased shares of stock in the company. In the desperate financial years of 2007, 2008, and now in 2009 Thoratec's revenues for fiscal 2008 increased 34% over their revenues in 2007.

Well, I hope this abbreviated book has been informative, educational, perhaps funny, and of help to all who have read it. I must say that Thoratec Corporation has prolonged my life. I would like to leave you with a spiritual message and that message is, if you understand the great plan of happiness and follow it, what goes on in this world at all times, as desperate as it seems, will not determine your happiness. You will be tried, for that is part of the plan, "but your afflictions shall be but a small moment, and then, if you endure it well, God shall exalt you on high." *

*Doctrine & Covenants 121: 7-8

My prayers are with all of you who suffer from congestive heart failure and any other afflictions. See your doctor, pray, be positive, and check out all of the heart assist devices available to you.

If you would like more information about the Plan of Salvation, please contact a representative from The Church of Jesus Christ of Latter-day Saints at 1-888-537-7700.

BONUS SOCIAL THOUGHTS

I wanted to share some of my feelings on the world and our own country. They are just some general ideas I think would be helpful at least to our country. If you disagree that's okay. But, if you agree, then vote for people who would bring these ideas to fruition. My following thoughts are not all inclusive, but they are a starter.

CONGRESS

We must pass an amendment to the United States constitution to limit congressmen to an eight-year term limit. We need to get rid of the professional, self-serving politicians, which have their own clubs, agendas, and serve each other rather than the people of the United States. A campaign expenditure of about four hundred thousand should also be placed on each candidate. This might make it more possible for the average

American to run for congress. There are too many millionaires in congress representing or caring about whom?

UNITED NATIONS

The United Nations should be relocated from New York City to Switzerland. This move would help keep more undesirables out of the country.

ILLEGAL IMMIGRANT

Illegal immigrants should receive no amnesty whatsoever when caught. They should receive a fine of $20,000 a person and five years in Sheriff Joe's Maricopa County, Arizona Test Prison. After serving the sentence of five years they should be deported. No matter where the illegals are caught they should still be retained in the custody of Sheriff Joe. Employers of illegal immigrants should be fined $100,000 per illegal person and their business closed for six months. Children of illegals born in this country are to be sent back to their home country, regardless of age.

CHINA

What can I say? We owe our financial soul to the Chinese. America has to bring our factories back from other countries. We have to highly tax goods made by U.S. companies in foreign lands and exported back to the United States. Congress should give better incentives to companies to stay in the U.S. And, yes, union people and stockholders get real, wages are too high, and dividend greed is too great. Let's do what's good for the country.

NORTH KOREA

This country's leaders are constantly trying to blackmail the United States with the threat of nuclear missiles, etc. The United States should provide South Korea with nuclear missiles for defensive purposes. The United States should always know where the North Korean top leadership is located and encourage citizens from within the country to overthrow them.

AFGHANISTAN

The United States should get out of Afghanistan. History tells us that there is never a winner in wars within this country. Use the money we now spend on the war for a Drug Defensive System to keep the narcotics out of other countries. Let them "pot" themselves to death if that is their choice. Let them resolve themselves to the kind of government they wish to have. It's not our business.

IRAQ

Thank goodness we are getting out of George W. Bush's personal vendetta war. We should only stay in Iraq with supervisory forces as long as they allow us to place military defense missiles in the country. Our defense would be of course against Iran. This defense system would be everlasting.

IRAN

The United States should leave them alone. Actually, who are we to tell other countries that they can't produce nuclear missiles, bombs, etc. when we have the ability to obliterate any country? We should employ a missile defense system in countries surrounding Iran free of charge.

GASOLINE & DIESEL FUELS

Raise the federal and state tax on fuels to provide for better roads, mass transportation, bridgework, etc. It would also force people to buy energy saving cars. Hopefully the American people would not go back to the big gas eaters. And, yes, the federal government should encourage people to buy fuel-efficient cars with a tax rebate. There should be no limitations on the number of cars eligible for the rebates.

MEDIA

There is a need for the media to investigate and constantly pound for change. Television news programs are so simple, never going in deep and getting at and preserving the truth.

ENERGY POLICY

Solar, Solar, Solar! Solar in the West, windmills would help for the rest of the states.

FOREIGN POLICY

Let's stay out of other countries unless we are wanted there and if only the United Nations is supporting the involvement. There is only one Savior for this world and it is not the United States government.

U.S. MAIL

Delivery three times a week is enough. Put up more group mailboxes instead of house-to-house stops. This may also help people with a little more exercise. Let's face it, with all the federal holidays and no mail delivery on those days, we have found we can "survive" without six day deliveries. It certainly would be money saving.

HEALTH CARE

Everyone that is a legal citizen in this country should have visual, dental, and general health care. When I was growing up we did not have money or health insurance to go to a doctor of any type. When I was teaching in Anchorage, Alaska during a Christmas vacation I had my long neglected dental care addressed. The school district didn't provide dental insurance, but I was earning enough money to pay for the dentistry. I had four wisdom teeth removed and if you can believe it, twenty-two cavities filled. Fortunately, I did not have pain through the years with my teeth being so neglected. However, I wonder if it had an influence on my heart problems.

Incidentally, the dentist who did the work on my teeth ended up in prison for manslaughter. He had about four dental recovery chairs for patients to sit in after he had done their dental work. The problem was he put patients to sleep with gas and some died unattended in the chairs. Well, that was Alaska in the 1960's. I was always blessed with great eyesight so I never needed to see an eye specialist.

I think without a doubt that the federal government has to exert more control over the medical profession and provide health care for all. We have a shortage of general practitioners right now because of poor decisions by physician training institutes and the American Medical Association (AMA). They felt some years ago that we had a surplus of doctors. So, to keep the fees up they put a freeze on the number of physicians to be trained. Well, of course, they were proved wrong.

The federal government needs to become involved in the training of doctors. More schools of medicine could be setup in various areas of the country. Government could help talented students with fees, tax benefits, etc. The AMA is too self-serving just like our congressmen. And, let's face it, does the required training for general practitioners have to be so long. I don't think so. Take a look at all the physician assistants who are doing the exact same work for the most part and are paid a lot less. How many general practitioners do surgery, or can diagnose correctly? Their patients are always referred to specialists when more specific medical help is needed.

The hospital charges should be looked at also. Recently, my wife was in the hospital for less than seven hours. She had a few general tests and was sent home. The bill was $10,000. Yes, $10,000! Hospitals that claim they are non-profit are probably the biggest deceivers in the country, Well, I could go on and on about health care and relate a lot of stories about it from my personal experiences, but you get the message.

Let's stop letting the AMA and training institutes have 100% control over medicine in the United States. No, I'm definitely not against physicians or hospitals, but in my mind they are the ones that are making health care unavailable to millions of people. And, let's not forget the benevolent drug companies. I say that as a joke on how they rip us off.

FEDERAL TAXES – PERSONAL

We should go to a flat tax tiered system. Only tax credits for medical expenses, charity, and energy saving products or structures (especially cars with no limits). For example, those earning ten thousand to thirty thousand dollars a year would pay 4%. Those making thirty-one thousand to fifty-one thousand dollars would pay a tax of 6%. Those earning from fifty-two thousand to eighty-two thousand would pay a 7% tax rate and so on. The percentage keeps climbing up to15% at the highest.

MISCELLANEOUS

I could go on and on about the economy, legal marriage, the scum and low morals demonstrated by TV and movie films, poor taste advertising, etc. But, it is so depressing. More integrity and much higher morals are needed to lift us out of the gutters of society. We each have to do more positive things in order to improve the quality of life in the United States and the world.

GLOSSARY*

If you've recently been diagnosed with advanced heart failure or are considering therapy options, you're probably hearing a lot of new terms. Talk to your doctor and consult this list to learn more.

- Advanced heart failure: A stage of heart failure in which therapies for earlier stages, such as optimal medical management with drugs, are not enough to provide enough heart function for the patient.
- Aorta: The main vessel exiting the heart, it carries blood from the left ventricle of the heart to arteries that provide blood flow to the rest of the body.
- Bi-VAD: Bi-Ventricular Assist Device, a VAD that can assist the function of either the right or the left side of the heart.
- Blood thinner: Medication used to prevent blood clots (for example, Coumadin or Lovenox).

- Bridge-to-transplantation (BTT): Temporary mechanical circulatory support (MCS) for advanced heart failure patients waiting for a donor heart to become available, BTT involves implantation of a ventricular assist device (VAD).
- Coronary Artery Bypass Grafting (CABG): Commonly called heart bypass, CABG is an open-heart surgery that reroutes (or 'bypasses') blood flow around blockages in the coronary arteries, restoring blood flow to the heart muscle.
- Cardiologist: Specialists in the structure, function and disorders of the heart, cardiologists are the first line of treatment for many heart failure patients. Heart failure cardiologists focus exclusively on patients with this condition.
- Cardiomyopathy: A disease in which an enlarged or damaged heart is severely weakened.
- Destination Therapy (DT): Long-term mechanical circulatory support for advanced heart failure patients who are not eligible for a heart transplant. Compare to Bridge-To-Transplantation Therapy.
- Edema: Swelling of soft tissues as a result of excess water accumulation. Edema can occur in almost any location in the body, but the most common sites are the feet and ankles.
- Ejection fraction: The efficiency with which the heart pumps blood, expressed in a percentage.
- Heart chambers: The four sections of the heart through which blood is pumped. The two upper chambers are called the left and right atria. The two lower chambers are the left and right ventricles. The right side of the heart receives oxygen-poor blood

from the body and pumps it to the lungs. The left side of the heart receives oxygen-rich blood from the lungs and pumps it to the rest of the body. The left ventricle performs 80% of the heart's work.

- Heart failure (HF): Also called congestive heart failure (CHF), a gradual weakening of the heart so that it cannot pump enough blood to the body's organs. Chronic conditions such as high blood pressure or blocked arteries can contribute to heart failure.
- Ischemic: Not receiving adequate blood flow.
- IVAD: Implantable Ventricular Assist Device.
- LVAD: Left Ventricular Assist Device.
- LVAS: Left Ventricle Assist System, which includes the LVAD (blood pump), and other system components (drive line, system controller, batteries, PBU and display module).
- Mechanical circulatory support (MCS): A way of improving blood flow using a ventricular assist device (VAD), which is an implantable, electrically powered heart pump that works to improve blood flow in cooperation with the heart. MCS is used either as Bridge-to-Transplantation therapy for heart failure patients awaiting heart transplant, or as Destination Therapy for patients ineligible for heart transplant. Additional uses include Post-Cardiotomy Recovery, for patients who are unable to wean from cardiopulmonary bypass, and short-term support for patients at risk of shock from acute heart failure while longer-term treatment decisions are being made.
- RVAD: Right Ventricular Assist Device.

- VAD: A ventricular assist device (VAD) is a heart pump designed to help restore proper pumping function to a weakened or damaged heart through a process called mechanical circulatory support (MCS). It works to improve blood flow in cooperation with your heart, but does not replace your own heart.
- VAD center: A medical center trained and equipped to implant ventricular assist devices (VADs) for the treatment of advanced heart failure. The VAD team consists of the VAD coordinator, cardiologist, cardiothoracic surgeon, and operating room and nursing staff.

*Reprinted with permission from the Thoratec Corporation.

LOCATIONS
OF LVAD CENTERS

Where are the Left Ventricular Assist Device (LVAD) centers in the United States? There are over 100 centers in the United States. They are listed here courtesy of the Thoratec Corporation.

Abbott Northwestern Hospital
Minneapolis, Minnesota

Albany Medical Center
Albany, New York

Allegheny General Hospital
Pittsburgh, Pennsylvania

Baptist Medical Center
Little Rock, Arkansas

Baptist Medical Oklahoma
Oklahoma City, Oklahoma

Baptist Memorial Hospital
Memphis, Tennessee

Barnes Jewish Hospital
St. Louis, Missouri

Baylor Medical Center
Dallas, Texas

Boston Medical Center
Boston, Massachusetts

Brigham and Women's Hospital
Boston, Massachusetts

Bryan LGH
Lincoln, Nebraska

California Pacific Medical Center
San Francisco, California

Carolinas Medical Center
Charlotte, North Carolina

Cedar Sinai Medical Center
Beverly Hills, California

Christ Medical Center
Oak Lawn, Illinois

Christus Santa Rosa Medical Center
San Antonio, Texas

Clarian Health
Indianapolis, Indiana

Cleveland Clinic Foundation
Cleveland, Ohio

Columbia Presbyterian Medical Center
New York, New York

Duke University Medical Center
Durham, North Carolina

Emory University Hospital
Atlanta, Georgia

Fairview University Medical Center/University of
Minnesota
Minneapolis, Minnesota

Froedtert Memorial Lutheran Hospital
Milwaukee, Wisconsin

Hahnemann University Hospital
Philadelphia, Pennsylvania

Hartford Hospital
Hartford, Connecticut

Henrico Doctor's Hospital
Richmond, Virginia

Henry Ford Hospital
Troy, Michigan

Hospital at the University of Pennsylvania
Philadelphia, Pennsylvania

Hunter Holmes Mcguire Veterans Affairs Medical Center
Richmond, Virginia

Inova Fairfax Hospital
Fairfax, Virginia

Intermountain Medical Center
Salt Lake City, Utah

Jewish Hospital
Louisville, Kentucky

Johns Hopkins University
Baltimore, Maryland

Kansas Heart Hospital
Wichita, Kansas

Lankenau Hospital
Wynnewood, Pennsylvania

Loma Linda Medical Center
Loma Linda, California

Loyola University Medical Center
Maywood, Illinois

Lutheran Hospital of Indiana
Fort Wayne, Indiana

Maine Medical Center
Portland, Maine

Massachusetts General Hospital
Charlestown, Massachusetts

Mayo Clinic
Rochester, Minnesota

Mayo Clinic Arizona
Phoenix, Arizona

Mayo Clinic Jacksonville
Jacksonville, Florida

Medical City Hospital of Dallas
Dallas, Texas

Medical College of Ohio
Toledo, Ohio

Medical College of Virginia Hospital
Richmond, Virginia

Medical University of South Carolina
Charleston, South Carolina

Methodist Hospital
Houston, Texas

Methodist Specialty & Transplant Hospital
San Antonio, Texas

Milton S. Hershey Medical Center
Hershey, Pennsylvania

Montefiore Medical Center
Bronx, New York

Nashville VA Medical Center
Nashville, Tennessee

New England Medical Center
Boston, Massachusetts

Newark Beth Israel Medical Center
Newark, New Jersey

North Shore University Hospital
Manhasset, New York

Northwestern Memorial Hospital
Chicago, Illinois

Ochsner Foundation Hospital
Jefferson, Louisiana

Ohio State University Medical Center
Columbus, Ohio

Oregon Health Sciences University
Portland, Oregon

Presbyterian Medical Center
Albuquerque, New Mexico

Providence Portland Medical Center
Portland, Oregon

Robert Wood Johnson University Hospital
New Brunswick, New Jersey

Rush Presbyterian Medical Center
Chicago, Illinois

Sacred Heart Medical Center
Spokane, Washington

Saint Francis Hospital
Tulsa, Oklahoma

Saint Joseph's Hospital
Atlanta, Georgia

Saint Luke's Health
Kansas City, Missouri

Sentara Norfolk Health System
Norfolk, Virginia

Seton Medical Center
Austin, Texas

Shands Hospital at the University of Florida
Gainesville, Florida

Sharp Memorial Hospital
San Diego, California

St. Francis Medical Center
Peoria, Illinois

St. Luke's Episcopal
Houston, Texas

St. Luke's Medical Center
Milwaukee, Wisconsin

St. Paul Medical Center
Dallas, Texas

St. Thomas Medical Center
Nashville, Tennessee

St. Vincent Medical Center
Los Angeles, California

St. Vincent's Hospital and Health Services of Indiana
Indianapolis, Indiana

Stanford Hospital and Clinic
Stanford, California

Tampa General Hospital
Tampa, Florida

Temple University Hospital
Philadelphia, Pennsylvania

Texas Heart Institute
Houston, Texas

The University Hospital
Cincinnati, Ohio

The University of Chicago Hospitals
Chicago, Illinois

The University of Iowa Hospitals and Clinics
Iowa City, Iowa

Tulane University
New Orleans, Louisiana

UCLA Medical Center
Los Angeles, California

UMass Medical School
Worcester, Massachusetts

University Hospitals of Cleveland
Cleveland, Ohio

University Medical Center
Tucson, Arizona

University of Alabama at Birmingham
Birmingham, Alabama

University of Arkansas
Little Rock, Arkansas

University of Colorado Health Sciences Center
Denver, Colorado

University of Kentucky Medical Center
Lexington, Kentucky

University of Miami – Jackson Memorial
Miami, Florida

University of Michigan Medical Center
Ann Arbor, Michigan

University of Missouri Hospital and Clinics
Columbia, Missouri

University of Nebraska Medical Center
Omaha, Nebraska

University of Pittsburgh Medical Center
Pittsburgh, Pennsylvania

University of Rochester Medical Center
Rochester, New York

University of Southern California
Los Angeles, California

University of Utah Health Sciences Center
Salt Lake City, Utah

University of Virginia Health Sciences Center
Charlottesville, Virginia

University of Washington Academic Medical Center
Seattle, Washington

University of Wisconsin Hospital and Clinics
Madison, Wisconsin

VA Medical Center
Salt Lake City, Utah

Via Christi Regional Medical Center
Wichita, Kansas

Washington Hospital Center
Washington D.C.

Westchester Medical Center
Valhalla, New York

Willis – Knighton Medical Center
Shreveport, Louisiana